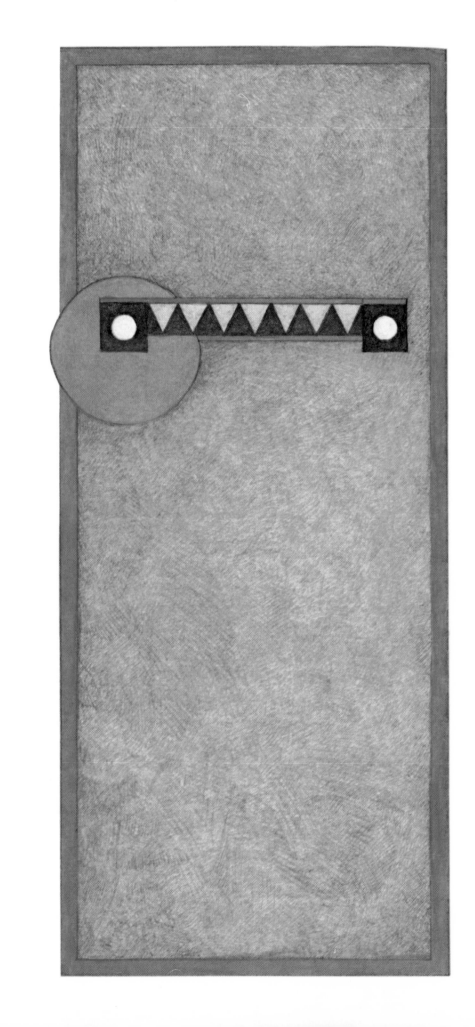

HE IS RISEN
The Easter Story

Adapted from The New Testament by

ELIZABETH WINTHROP

illustrated by

CHARLES MIKOLAYCAK

Holiday House/New York

Library of Congress Cataloging in Publication data

Winthrop, Elizabeth.
    He is risen.

    Summary: An adaptation of the Bible story of Christ's
Crucifixion and Resurrection.
    1. Jesus Christ—Resurrection—Biblical teaching—
Juvenile literature. [1. Jesus Christ—Crucifixion.
2. Jesus Christ—Resurrection. 3. Bible stories—N.T.
4. Easter] I. Mikolaycak, Charles, ill. II. Bible. N.T.
Matthew. Selections.   III. Bible. N.T. Luke. Selections.
IV. Title.
BT480.A3   1985   226'.09505   84-15869
ISBN 0-8234-0547-8

He Is Risen: The Easter Story is adapted from the Book of St. Matthew, 26:1–5, 14–30, 34–45, 47–49, 55–67, 69–75; 27: 1–8, 11–17, 21–42, 45–46, 48–60, 62–66; 28:1–3, 5–10, 16–20, and the Book of St. Luke, 22:48; 23:34, 39–40, 42–43, in the King James Version of the Bible. The author has remained faithful to the Biblical text, both in punctuation and in spelling. But with a young audience in mind, she has simplified some of the vocabulary and omitted certain passages.

And it came to pass that Jesus said unto his disciples, Ye know that after two days is the feast of the passover, and the Son of man is betrayed to be crucified.

Then the chief priests, and the scribes, and the elders of the people gathered together in the palace of the high priest and consulted with one another that they might take Jesus secretly and kill him.

But they said, Not on the feast day, lest there be an uproar among the people.

Then one of the twelve disciples, called Judas Iscariot, went unto the chief priests,

And said unto them, What will ye give me if I deliver Jesus unto you? And they made a bargain with him for thirty pieces of silver.

And from that time on Judas sought to betray Jesus.

Now the first day of the feast of unleavened bread the disciples came to Jesus, saying unto him, Where will thou have us prepare for thee to eat the passover?

And he said, Go into the city to such a man, and say unto him, The Master says, My time is at hand; I will keep the passover at thy house with my disciples.

And the disciples did as Jesus had told them; and they made ready the passover.

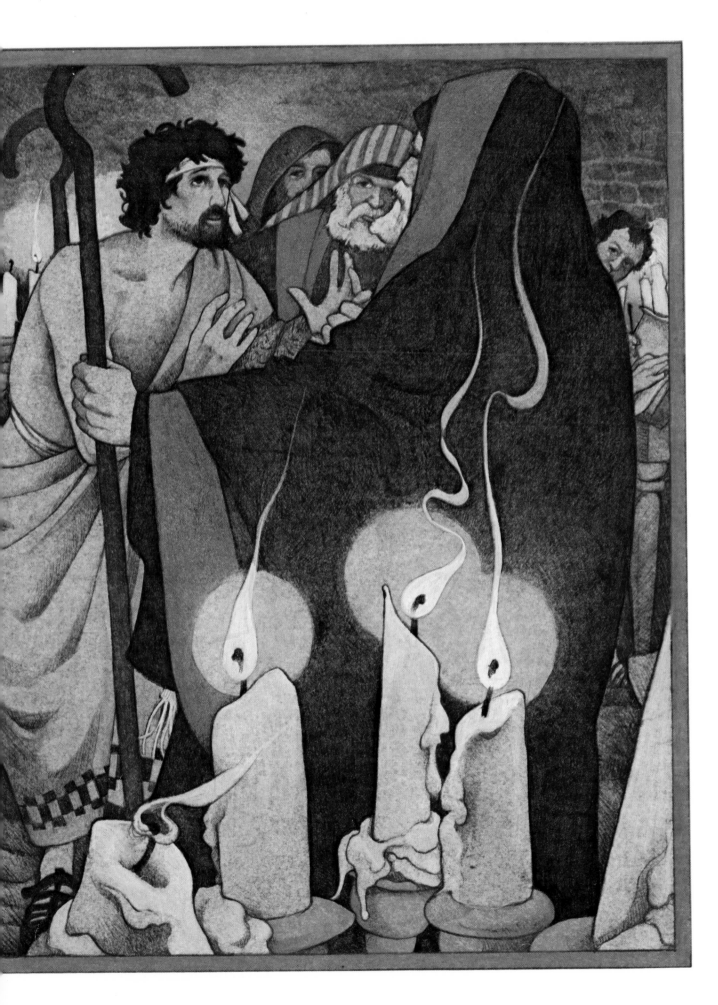

Now when the evening was come, Jesus sat down with the twelve.

And as they did eat, he said, Verily I say unto you, that one of you shall betray me.

And they were very sad, and began every one of them to say unto him, Lord, is it I?

And he answered and said, He that dips his hand with me in the dish, the same shall betray me.

Woe unto that man by whom the Son of man is betrayed! it would be better for that man if he had not been born.

Then Judas said, Master, is it I?

Jesus answered, Thou hast said it.

And as they were eating, Jesus took bread, and blessed it, and broke it, and gave it to the disciples, and said, Take, eat; this is my body.

And he took the cup, and gave thanks, and gave it to them, saying, Drink ye all of this;

For this is my blood of the new testament, which is shed for many for the forgiveness of sins.

But I say unto you, I will not drink henceforth of this fruit of the vine, until that day when I drink it new with you in my Father's kingdom.

And when they had sung an hymn, they went out to the mount of Olives.

Then Jesus said unto Peter, Verily I say unto thee, That this night, before the cock crow, thou shalt deny me three times.

Peter said unto him, Though I should die with thee, yet will I not deny thee. Likewise said all the disciples.

Then Jesus came with them unto a place called Gethsemane, and said unto the disciples, Sit ye here, while I go and pray yonder.

And he took with him Peter and the two sons of Zebedee, and began to be sorrowful and very troubled.

Then he said unto them, My soul is sorrowful, even unto death: stay ye here, and watch with me.

And he went a little farther, and fell on his face, and prayed, saying, O my Father, if it be possible, let this cup pass from me: nevertheless let not my will, but thine be done.

And he came back to the disciples, and finding them asleep, he said unto Peter, What, could ye not watch with me one hour?

Watch and pray: the spirit indeed is willing, but the flesh is weak.

He went away again the second time, and prayed, saying, O my Father, if this cup may not pass away from me, unless I drink it, thy will be done.

And he came and found them asleep again: for their eyes were heavy.

And he left them, and went away again, and prayed the third time, saying the same words.

Then he came to his disciples, and said unto them, Sleep on now, and take your rest: behold, the hour is at hand, and the Son of man is betrayed into the hands of sinners.

And while he spoke, Judas came, and with him a great multitude with swords and staves, that had been sent from the chief priests and elders of the people.

Now Judas had said to them, Whomsoever I shall kiss, that same is Jesus: hold him fast.

And forthwith he came to Jesus, and said, Hail, master; and kissed him.

And Jesus said unto him, Judas, dost thou betray the Son of man with a kiss?

Then came the multitude and laid hands on Jesus and took him. In that same hour, Jesus turned and said, Are ye come out as ye would against a thief with swords and staves to take me? I sat daily with you teaching in the temple, and ye did not lay hold of me.

But all this was done, that the scriptures of the prophets might be fulfilled. Then all the disciples forsook him, and fled.

And they that held Jesus led him away to Caiaphas the high priest, where the scribes and the elders were gathered.

Peter followed him from afar to the high priest's palace, and went in, and sat with the servants, to see the end.

Now the chief priests, and elders, and all the council, sought false witnesses against Jesus, to put him to death;

At last came forward two false witnesses,

And said, This fellow said, I am able to destroy the temple of God, and to rebuild it in three days.

And the high priest arose, and said unto Jesus, Answerest thou nothing?

But Jesus held his peace. And the high priest said unto him, I charge thee by the living God, that thou tell us whether thou be the Christ, the Son of God.

Jesus saith unto him, Thou hast said it: nevertheless I say unto you, Hereafter shall ye see the Son of man sitting on the right hand of power, and coming in the clouds of heaven.

Then the high priest tore his clothes, saying, Behold, now ye have heard his blasphemy.

What think ye? They answered and said, He is guilty of death.

Then did they spit in his face, and buffeted him; and others struck him with the palms of their hands.

Now Peter sat in the outer part of the palace: and a damsel came unto him, saying, Thou also was with Jesus of Galilee.

But he denied it before them all, saying, I know not what thou sayest.

And when he was gone out of the gate, another maid saw him, and said unto them that were there, This fellow was also with Jesus of Nazareth.

And again he denied it with an oath, saying, I do not know the man.

And after a while they that stood by came unto Peter and said to him, Surely thou also art one of them; for thy speech betrayeth thee.

Then Peter began to curse and to swear, saying, I know not the man. And immediately the cock crew.

And Peter remembered the words that Jesus had said, Before the cock crow, thou shalt deny me three times. And Peter went out, and wept bitterly.

When the morning was come, all the chief priests and elders bound Jesus and led him away, and delivered him to Pontius Pilate the governor.

Then Judas, who had betrayed him, when he saw that Jesus was condemned, repented, and brought again the thirty pieces of silver to the chief priests and elders,

Saying, I have sinned in that I have betrayed innocent blood. And they said, What is that to us? see thou to that.

And Judas cast down the pieces of silver in the temple, and went away, and hanged himself.

And the chief priests took the silver pieces, and with them they bought the potter's field, to bury strangers in.

And unto this day that field is called, The field of blood.

And Jesus stood before the governor: and the governor asked him, saying, Art thou the King of the Jews? And Jesus answered unto him, Thou sayest it.

And when he was accused by the chief priests and elders, he answered nothing.

Then Pilate said unto him, Dost thou not hear how many things they charge against thee?

But Jesus answered him never a word, and the governor marveled greatly.

Now at that feast it was the custom for the governor to release unto the people a prisoner, whomever they desired.

And they had then a well-known prisoner, called Barabbas.

Therefore when the people were gathered together, Pilate said unto them, Whom shall I release unto you? Barabbas, or Jesus who is called Christ?

They said, Barabbas.

Pilate said unto them, What shall I do then with Jesus? They all said unto him, Let him be crucified.

And the governor said, Why, what evil has he done? But they cried out the more, saying, Let him be crucified.

When Pilate saw that he could do nothing, he took water, and washed his hands before the multitude, saying, I am innocent of the blood of this just person: see ye to it.

Then answered all the people, His blood be on us, and on our children.

Then Pilate released Barabbas unto them: and when he had whipped Jesus, he delivered him to be crucified.

Then the soldiers took Jesus into the common hall,

And they stripped him, and put on him a scarlet robe.

And when they had braided a crown of thorns, they put it upon his head, and a reed in his right hand: and they bowed before him and mocked him, saying, Hail, King of the Jews!

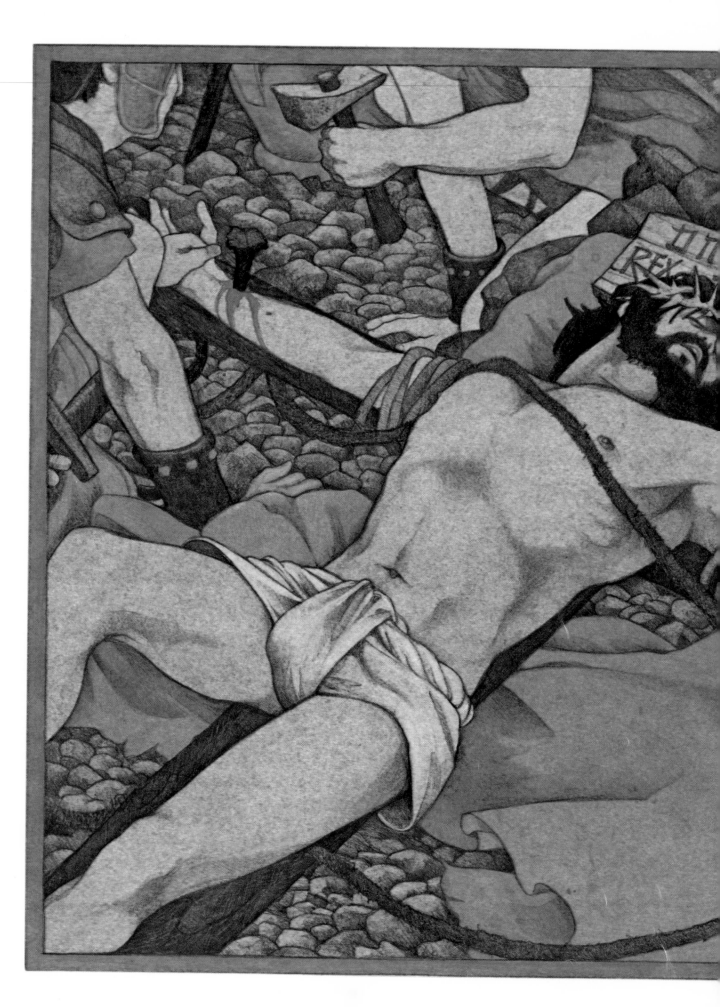

And they spit upon him, and took the reed, and struck him on the head.

And after they had mocked him, they took the robe off him, and put his own garments on him, and led him away to crucify him.

And as they came out, they found a man of Cyrene, Simon by name: and they forced him to take up Jesus's cross.

And when they came unto a place called Golgotha,

They gave him vinegar mixed with gall: and when he had tasted it, he would not drink it.

And they crucified him, and divided his garments, among them, casting lots.

And sitting down they watched him there;

And set up over his head the charge against him, written, THIS IS JESUS THE KING OF THE JEWS.

Then said Jesus, Father, forgive them; for they know not what they do.

And they that passed by jeered at him, wagging their heads,

And saying, Thou that destroyed the temple, and rebuilt it in three days, save thyself. If thou be the Son of God, come down from the cross.

Likewise also the chief priests with the scribes and elders, mocked him, saying,

He saved others: but himself he cannot save. If he be the King of Israel, let him now come down from the cross, and we will believe him.

Then were there two thieves crucified with him, one on the right hand, and another on the left.

And one of the thieves reproached him, saying, If thou be Christ, save thyself and us.

But the other answering, rebuked him, saying, Dost not thou fear God, seeing thou art under the same condemnation?

And he said unto Jesus, Lord, remember me when thou comest into thy kingdom.

And Jesus said unto him, Verily, I say unto thee, Today shalt thou be with me in paradise.

Now from the sixth hour there was darkness over all the land unto the ninth hour.

And about the ninth hour Jesus cried out with a loud voice, saying, *Eli, Eli, lama sabachthani?* that is to say, My God, my God, why hast thou forsaken me?

And straightaway one of them ran, and took a sponge, and filled it with vinegar, and put it on a reed, and gave it to him to drink.

The rest said, Let him be, let us see whether Elias will come to save him.

Jesus, when he had cried out again with a loud voice, yielded up the ghost.

And, behold, the curtain of the temple was torn in two from the top to the bottom; and the earth did quake, and the rocks split;

And the graves were opened; and many bodies of the saints which slept arose,

And came out of the graves and went into the holy city, and appeared unto many.

Now when the centurion, and they that were with him, watching Jesus, saw the earthquake, and those things that were done, they feared greatly, saying, Truly this was the Son of God.

And many women who had followed Jesus from Galilee were there watching from afar.

Among them were Mary Magdalene, and Mary the mother of James and Joseph, and the mother of Zebedee's children.

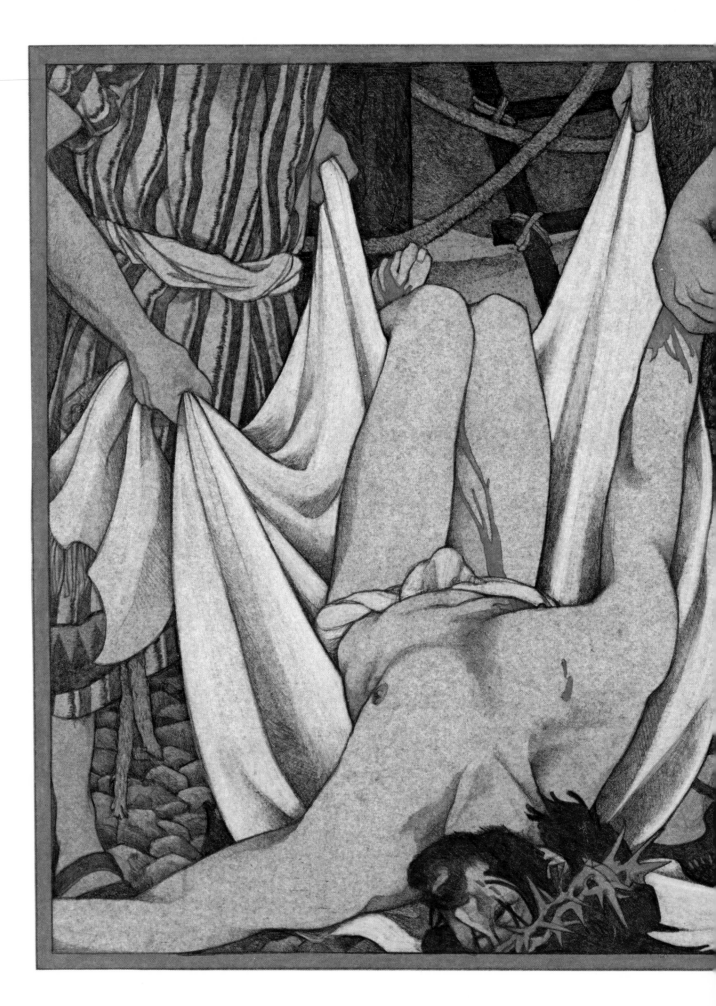

When it was evening, there came a rich man of Arimathaea, named Joseph, who also himself was a disciple of Jesus;

He went to Pilate, and begged for the body of Jesus. Then Pilate commanded the body to be delivered.

And when Joseph had taken the body, he wrapped it in a clean linen cloth,

And laid it in his own new tomb, which he had cut out in the rock: and he rolled a great stone to the door of the sepulchre, and departed.

Now the next day, the chief priests and Pharisees came together unto Pilate,

Saying, Sir, we remember that the deceiver said, while he was yet alive, After three days I will rise again.

Command therefore that the sepulchre be guarded until the third day, lest his disciples come by night, and steal him away, and say unto the people, He is risen from the dead.

Pilate said unto them, Ye have a watch: go your way, make it as sure as you can.

So they went, sealing the stone and setting a watch.

On the first day of the week, near the end of the Sabbath, Mary Magdalene and the other Mary came to see the sepulchre.

And, behold, there was a great earthquake: for the angel of the Lord descended from heaven, and rolled back the stone from the door, and sat upon it.

His countenance was like lightning, and his garment white as snow:

And the angel said unto the women, Fear not ye: for I know that ye seek Jesus, who was crucified.

He is not here: for he is risen, as he said. Come, see the place where the Lord lay.

And go quickly, and tell his disciples that he is risen from the dead; and, behold, he goes before you into Galilee; and there shall ye find him.

And they departed quickly from the sepulchre with fear and great joy.

And as they went to tell his disciples, Jesus met them, saying, All hail. And the women held him by the feet and worshipped him.

Then said Jesus unto them, Be not afraid: go tell my brethren that if they go into Galilee, there shall they see me.

Then the eleven disciples went away into Galilee.

And when they saw Jesus, they worshipped him, but some doubted.

And Jesus spoke unto them, saying, All power is given unto me in heaven and on earth.

Go ye therefore, and teach all nations, baptizing them in the name of the Father, and of the Son, and of the Holy Ghost.

Teach them to observe all things whatsoever I have commanded you: and, lo, I am with you always, even unto the end of the world.

The book was set in 14 point Janson (CRT) type.
Typography by David Rogers.

The illustrations were completed by applying watercolors and colored pencils to Diazo prints made same size from the original pencil drawings.

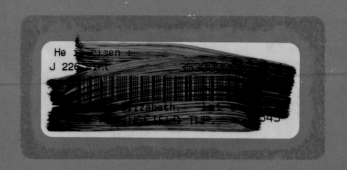